JERRY YANG

CHIEF YAHOO

BY CAROLINE LEAVITT

For Jeff and Max with all my love
—C. L.

Photo credits: cover and title page: © Paul Sakuma/AP Wide World; cover headshot: © courtesy of Yahoo!; p. 5: © Segar/Reuters/NewsCom; p. 6: © Jack Fields/CORBIS; p. 7: © Charles O'Rear/CORBIS; p. 9: © Classmates.com; p. 11: © Robert Holmgren/Zuma/NewsCom; p. 12: © Chuck Painter/Stanford University News Service; p. 13: © Owen Franken/CORBIS; p. 14: © Gianni Giansanti/Sygma/CORBIS; p. 15 © Yoshikazu Tsuno/AFP/Getty Images; pp. 17, 18: © Scott Barbour/Getty Images; p. 19: © AP Wide World; p. 20: © Romeo Gacad/AFP Getty Images; p. 21: © Ed Kashi/CORBIS; p. 22: Time & Life Pictures/Getty Images; p. 23: © Francis Dean/The Image Works; p. 24: © Clark Jones/AP Wide World; p. 25: © Paul Sakuma/Associated Press, AP; p. 27: © Business Wire/Getty Images; p. 28: Mario Jose Sanchez/Associated Press, AP

For information contact: MONDO Publishing,

980 Avenue of the Americas, New York, NY 10018

Visit our website at http://www.mondopub.com

Printed in China

07 08 09 10 11   9 8 7 6 5 4 3 2 1

ISBN 1-59336-771-6

Designed by E. Friedman

Contents

INTRODUCTION

Jerry Yang sits in his yellow and purple office, playing on a computer. He hasn't slept at all, and his hair is rumpled. He's wearing his usual casual clothing—blue jeans, T-shirt, and sneakers. Lively sounds come from another room—a wild Frisbee match, probably run by his friend David Filo. Jerry Yang looks like a college kid having a good time, but he is actually one of the wealthiest men in the world. Despite the low-key atmosphere in his office, he is also one of the hardest-working and most dedicated innovators around. Jerry Yang helped create Yahoo!, an Internet company that took the world by storm. And he did it by following his dreams.

CHAPTER 1
Becoming Jerry Yang

Jerry Yang wasn't always Jerry Yang. When he was born in 1968 in Taipei, the capital city of Taiwan (pictured above), he was given the Chinese name Yang Chih-Yuan. (Chinese names are always in reverse order; that is, the last name, or family name, is written first, and the first name is written last.) Chih-Yuan's mother, a drama and language professor, was Taiwanese, but his father had immigrated to Taiwan from mainland China. When Chih-Yuan was one year old, his parents had a second child—a new baby boy! But the family's happiness was short-lived. When Chih-Yuan was just two, his father died suddenly. His mother was left to care for Chih-Yuan and his baby brother completely on her own.

With Chih-Yuan's father gone, life wasn't easy for the Yang family. Yet right from the start, young Chih-Yuan seemed destined to excel. From the time he could speak, he was always asking questions. He was curious about everything and everyone. His mother was happy to explain things to him, and by the time Chih-Yuan was three, he was already reading and writing.

Yang Chih-Yuan was too young to understand how difficult the situation was for his mother. Although she was a teacher, there weren't many jobs open for women in Taiwan during that time, and money was very tight. She didn't know if she could earn enough to support her family. Also, she looked to the future and was worried that when her sons were older, they would be forced into Taiwan's mandatory military service before they had a chance to be fully educated. At that time, many people in Taiwan were emigrating to the United States, where there seemed to be more opportunities. In 1978, when Chih-Yuan was ten, his mother packed up her small family and moved to America. They settled in sunny San Jose, California, in the heart of the "Silicon Valley"—an area famous for its innovative, high-tech business.

An aerial view of "Silicon Valley"

Chih-Yuan's mother felt that a new country warranted a whole new outlook—and new names. She thought Jerry was a much more American-sounding name, which is how Yang Chih-Yuan became Jerry Yang. His younger brother took the name Ken Yang, and their mother changed her name to Lily Yang. She became an English and drama professor at a nearby San Jose college. Jerry thought his mother was very brave to come to a new country and get a job teaching in a language that was not her native tongue. She made him feel proud.

Jerry knew only one word in English when he arrived in America: *shoe*. So it wasn't easy for Jerry and Ken when they first started school. They were often teased for looking different from everyone else and for not speaking the language very well. At first Jerry was mystified by American money. Who was that strange-looking guy on the dollar bill? But even when he was still learning the ins and outs of American culture, one thing he could always do better than the other kids was math. When it came to math tests, Jerry always got As, something that impressed the other kids and boosted his status. In just a few years, Jerry and Ken moved from remedial reading classes into Advanced Placement English classes. Jerry soon began excelling in other subjects and continued to do so throughout high school.

When he attended Piedmont Hills High School, Jerry began taking even more Advanced Placement courses. He took so many of these advanced classes that he would later have enough credits to skip his freshman year at college! In high school, Jerry became so popular that he was called a BMOC, which is an acronym for "big man on campus." Elected president of the student body, he also played on the school's tennis team, and he even delivered the valedictory speech at graduation.

Jerry had many scholarship offers, including one from Caltech (the California Institute of Technology), but he decided to go to Stanford University in Palo Alto so that he could live near his family. He also appreciated that Stanford, unlike many other colleges, didn't force him to declare a major right away. "I thought I wanted to be an electrical engineer, which I turned out to be," Jerry said. "But I was always curious about other things, too, and what if I got interested in history or the law?" At Stanford Jerry studied electrical engineering and worked part-time at the library,

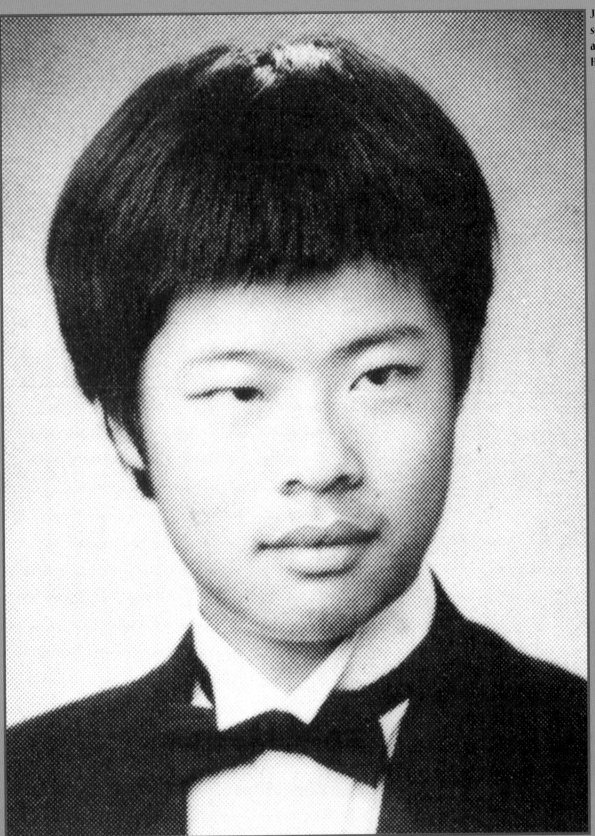

sorting and shelving books. "That's where I first learned about how systematically information was categorized—you know, the Dewey decimal system and all that," Jerry said.[1] This knowledge of categorization would later come in very handy—when he started working with computers.

A straight-A student, Jerry finished both his bachelor's and master's degrees at Stanford in just four years. (It usually takes five to six.) In 1990 he began studying for his Ph.D. in electrical engineering. It seemed as though Jerry could accomplish any goal.

CHAPTER 2
Jerry Meets His Match

Did you ever feel that you could go twice as far if you had a partner to help you? Maybe it was fate that Jerry met David Filo. David grew up in Louisiana and earned his bachelor's degree in computer engineering at Tulane University. When he went to Stanford to study electrical engineering, he and Jerry attended many of the same classes. They both loved computers, so it made sense that they'd become friends. Another common bond was that they were both having trouble completing their theses, major research projects that sometimes take years to finish. Jerry was writing about making computer chips, but he wasn't very excited by the project. But very soon, all that was going to change.

In the 1990s, more and more people were buying home computers and discovering what exciting tools they could be. Many were growing to love the Internet, where it was possible to get all kinds of fascinating information and chat with people all over the world. The Internet was turning into an important resource. And even better, it was just plain fun.

One day in 1993, Jerry and David were lazing around in a trailer that housed their computers on the Stanford campus, looking for a way to avoid working on their theses. Surfing the web seemed like the perfect distraction! So both young men began looking at the new, exciting websites that were popping up all over the Internet. There were websites devoted to sports, websites about movies, and sites about cooking—even sites that honed in on very particular subjects, such as a certain breed of dogs. What really interested Jerry and David were basketball scores and sumo wrestlers. They used the Internet to track National Basketball Association scores and read about their favorite sumo wrestlers. But how did they find and get to these sites?

Computers have what is called a browser. That's the software that lets

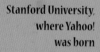
Stanford University, where Yahoo! was born

Computers have come a long way since the early 1990s.

you go to different websites, or pages, on the Internet. The problem was that in those days, once you left or closed a page, there was no easy way to bookmark it or find it again if you wanted to go back to it. You had to write down the web address, or URL (Uniform Resource Locator), to find your favorite sites in the future. You could end up with pages and pages of addresses. And it was difficult to keep track of the information found on each site.

Jerry and David decided it would be helpful to make a list of their favorite sites. "Really, we'd do anything to keep from working on our theses," Jerry said.[2] They began typing in their personal favorites, a hotlist of places they always returned to. And they created links to each of their favorite sites. (Links are highlighted words or images that are references to other web pages or documents.) That way they could just click on a link and go right to that site.

Before long, the list began to grow, so Jerry and David began dividing the sites into categories, such as sports and movies. When those categories got too full, they then made sub-categories—for example, basketball and baseball for sports, and westerns and dramas for movies. Jerry put up his own web page, too, one that contained his name in

Chinese, his golf scores, and Jerry and David's list of their favorite sites. Soon the two friends were spending more time on the web than on their theses, but the best thing about it was that instead of being bored, they were finally fired up and having fun.

Jerry and David wanted their friends to benefit, too, so they created a combined web page and posted their lists of sites on their computer workstation at Stanford. Internet users could log on to this web page and access any site on the list by clicking on the desired link. Word quickly

Jerry and David at work in their laid-back office environment

began to spread, and within six months of the site's debut, the number of hits (times the site was accessed) doubled. Then it soon tripled.

The two Ph.D. students named their website "Jerry and David's Guide to the World Wide Web," but neither one really liked the name. It was too long and not at all catchy or amusing. This was a problem since both Jerry and David loved fun-sounding names. They had named their computers after legendary sumo wrestlers: David's computer was called Konishiki, while Jerry had named his computer Akebono. Surely their new venture deserved a great name, too—a name that was smart and playful, and would make people smile.

Jerry and David combed through dictionaries and racked their brains trying to come up with just the right name. And suddenly there in the dictionary, they found it: Yahoo! Yahoo has several different meanings. It originally comes from Jonathan Swift's 18th-century book, Gulliver's Travels. When the main character, Gulliver, arrived at the land of the Houyhnhnm, he encountered intelligent horses who viewed any human as a Yahoo—a rude, unsophisticated being. Jerry and David also coined the acronym YAHOO—Yet Another Hierarchical Officious Oracle. (This was a funny way of saying that their website was a meddling ranking system that delivered clever and helpful information!) And finally, as many people know, shouting "Yahoo!" is another way of saying "hooray."

1 yahoo \yä ˈhü\ n., pl **yahoos** (1726) 1 *cap*: one of a race of brutes in Jonathan Swift's *Gulliver's Travels* who have the form and all of the vices of humans 2 a boorish, crude, or unintelligent person
2 yahoo \yä ˈhü\ interj used to attract attention [YIPPEE]

Jerry and David weren't advertising their site, but word kept spreading. In one online interview, Jerry said. "Through most of 1994, even though we were playing with Yahoo!…[t]here was no real business model that fit it. For example, we knew we had to keep it free because everything on the

Jerry named his computer after this sumo wrestler, Yokozuna Akebono.

Internet was free. So there was no way to charge people for using it or even to charge people for their sites to be listed on it. And besides, we were just two guys slaving away on the technology. What did we know?"[3]

In 1994 Yahoo! had a million hits. Jerry and David were thrilled, but Stanford wasn't pleased. "They told us we were crashing their system and that we'd have to move the thing off campus," Jerry said.[4] Jerry and David were hopeful but not certain that their website might be the seeds of a successful business. In early 1995, the two students—still registered at Stanford—moved off campus and focused completely on Yahoo! Well maybe not completely. That same year Jerry and Akiko Yamazaki, a Japanese-American raised in Costa Rica, got married!

CHAPTER 3
Do You Yahoo?

Running a business often requires many people, but at the beginning it was just Jerry and David. "Thousands of people were producing new websites every day," David said. "We were just trying to take all that stuff and organize it to make it useful. And as it became more popular, it became pretty clear we would have to get more people involved."[5] But who?

Jerry had a friend, Tim Brady, who was attending Harvard University. For a class project, Tim had to write a business plan—a detailed outline that shows the way a business is going to run. Generally when people want to start a business, they need to show a business plan to prospective investors. If the business plan is carefully thought out and the new business looks like it will make money, the prospective investors may lend the people money to start and run the business. As his project, Tim Brady wrote a business plan for Jerry and David, and he did it for free. They never actually used the plan, but they did hire their friend as Yahoo!'s third employee.

In March 1995, with their theses still unfinished, both Jerry and David took leaves of absence from school to devote themselves full-time to Yahoo! "It was really, really hard to [leave school]," Jerry said. "I'm not a quitter."[6]

Jerry and David needed money to turn Yahoo! into a real business. They met with several venture capital companies, including Sequoia Capital, an investment firm that gave them two million dollars to fund their business. Suddenly Yahoo! was off and running. Now that they had money from investors, Jerry and David wanted to manage their new company so it could grow. To do that, they needed to hire people to help them. By 1996

Yahoo! had 49 employees.

Although Jerry and David were no longer studying at Stanford, they still remained connected to their college beginnings. Another young Stanford graduate who joined the company early on was Srinija Srinivasan. She was in charge of organizing the growing number of topics and sub-topics that Yahoo! used to categorize websites. Yahoo! has key categories, such as Arts, Business, Entertainment, Health, and Science, that help Internet users find what they're looking for on the web.

Jerry and David hired another Stanford graduate, Tim Koogle, to act as their president and CEO (chief executive officer). Koogle had led other high-tech companies, and Yahoo! seemed like a wonderful new challenge. "When I first met Jerry and David," Koogle said in an interview, "what struck me immediately was that they had filled a fundamental need and they had done it intuitively. That's what you look for in starting a business."[7]

Like with any company, Yahoo! occasionally had problems. Netscape had made Yahoo! its number one link on its directory page. Yahoo! had helped make Netscape's browser more popular because Netscape users could easily link to the many great Yahoo! pages. But when Netscape was offered more money from a new search engine, they bumped Yahoo! from their page in favor of Yahoo!'s competitor. Jerry and David could easily have become angry, but they didn't. With Koogle as an advisor, the undaunted pair decided to continue to concentrate on what they had always done, which was to create the best possible online directory. Not surprisingly the traffic on their website dropped when Yahoo! was first bumped from Netscape, but to their amazement, the number of hits began climbing again and continued to climb. Netscape eventually put Yahoo! back up on its directory.

With Koogle at the helm, the company was able to "go public" in 1996. That meant that people could buy stock in the company, thus generating

Excitement is in the air as trading begins on Yahoo! stock, September 9, 1997.

more funds for Yahoo! Soon more than 100 people had come to work at Yahoo! to categorize websites, sell advertising, and help manage the company—and there were more than 300 advertisers.

All Yahoo! employees believed that the Internet should be free whenever possible. "We're not in this for the fast money," Jerry said.[8] But of course all businesses need to make money to survive, so Yahoo! continually had to find sponsors and advertisers. This enabled Yahoo! to continue to provide a free service to its users.

Why did Yahoo! do such great business? It was simple to use, and it made the Internet easy to navigate. Visitors would go to the site (http://www.Yahoo.com) and type a word into the query box and click on it. The query could be anything from Bill Clinton to tyrannosaurs to basketball. Yahoo! has a computer program that combs its own database, along with other search engines, until it locates web pages, texts, and URLs that have a specific word or string of words in it. The results pop up and are ranked in order of importance.

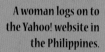

A woman logs on to the Yahoo! website in the Philippines.

David and Jerry relax with a game of foosball.

Working at Yahoo wasn't like working at any other company. Yahoo!'s purple and yellow colors were everywhere—on the furniture and on the walls. No one wore suits and ties—unless they really wanted to. It was a lot like a group of friends in a college dorm working together on something they loved. Yes, there were long hours of hard work, and the job required a lot of dedication, but there were also Frisbee matches and roller hockey games. "Every person who decided to join Yahoo!" Jerry told an interviewer, "has had the notion that by being part of this organization, they can change the world."[9] Though Internet companies struggled to remain competitive at the beginning of the new century, Yahoo! survived those turbulent days. There was something appealing about the company because it seemed so young and fresh, and everyone working there was so excited by what was going on.

Because the company was so successful, Jerry and David were asked by both Netscape and AOL (formerly America Online) whether they wanted to sell the company. Netscape is a company that provides software for browsing information on the Internet. AOL is in part an Internet service provider (ISP), a company that provides access to the Internet. Jerry and

JULY 20, 1998 $2.95

www.time.co

TIME

KISS YOUR MALL GOODBYE

Jerry Yang
of Yahoo!

**Online shopping is faster,
cheaper and better**

Plus: Hot stocks and brash billionaires

David could have walked away from the high stress of their business with millions of dollars in the bank and a reputation as whiz kids, but they held fast to their principles and refused to sell. It wasn't money but the thrill of doing something interesting and innovative that drove them.

In 1998 *PC Magazine* named Jerry Yang and David Filo "People of the Year," and the magazine called Yahoo! "a full-featured one-stop web center that can occupy its visitors for an entire day." When interviewed by *Time* magazine that same year, Jerry was as amusing and insightful as always. "My favorite thing to do when I'm not working is sleeping," he said. He also told *Time* that one day he expected the Internet to be as common as TV and the telephone—a very accurate prediction!

To stay competitive, Jerry and David decided they needed to advertise and soon came up with some creative advertisements that were as fresh and fun as the company. Their slogan was "Do You Yahoo!?" One ad showed a ragged-looking punk rocker searching for a quilting group to join—an unlikely hobby for that sort of musician. Another famous ad, known as "Superhero," showed a haggard, out-of-shape comic-book hero who wasn't strong enough to stop a purse snatcher. He felt so guilty about his failure to live up to everyone's expectations that he turned to Yahoo! to buy

A taxi van in Denmark advertises Yahoo!

replacement purses for the victims. The message of these ads was that one could find anything on Yahoo!

Always innovative, in 2006 Yahoo! held a Man vs. Monkey Technology Challenge—a race to see whether humans or chimpanzees could shoot and print a digital image faster. The event was held to promote Yahoo! Tech, a website that makes technology easy to understand.

Even a monkey can understand how to use Yahoo!'s instructions.

CHAPTER 4
Yahoo! Today

Today Yahoo! is a leading global communications, commerce, and media company, and it's the most trafficked Internet destination in the world. It has its headquarters, pictured above, in Sunnyvale, California, but there are also offices in Europe, Asia, Latin America, Australia, Canada, and elsewhere in the United States. And it's still a free service for Internet users.

How has success personally affected Jerry Yang? Well, by the age of 30 he was worth over three billion dollars and could easily retire. Yet he still continues to work really hard every day. This Chief Yahoo! (his official company title) sometimes even works all night and sleeps in the office. Jerry loves what he does and plans to continue doing it as long as it's enjoyable. He admires people like Michael Dell, the founder of Dell computers. "I look at people who've gone through a lot of adversity and are still great leaders in their field," he says.[10] Perhaps that's because Jerry remembers how hard it was for his mother to move her whole family from Taiwan to a new country, and how he and his brother also had to struggle at first before they could succeed.

Yahoo! today is bigger than ever and has additional products to serve different populations. There's Yahoo! Sports, Yahoo! Music, Yahoo! Shopping, and free e-mail. There's national news, weather, stock quotes, and ways to find an apartment. Want to play games online, upload videos, or chat? Yahoo! has that for you, too. There's even a kids' web guide called Yahooligans! The chair and CEO since 2001, Terry Semel, helps keep the company focused and growing. Today Yahoo! attracts more than 345 million users each month.

In 2005 the Yahoo! web directory listed over 1 million sites. To stay up-to-date, Yahoo! is continually adding new listings. The company gets a lot more suggested listings than it can handle, so it tries to find the sites that will offer the best benefits to the most people. The people that Yahoo! hires to be "surfers" are always on the lookout for interesting and unusual sites.

Yahoo! is also committed to making a difference in the world. It uses its products and services to connect people with worthwhile causes such as Yahoo! Missing Children Alerts—one of their community relations programs. Yahoo! also has partnerships with nonprofit organizations like the American Red Cross and Big Brothers Big Sisters, as well as an employee foundation that donates millions of dollars in grants to organizations around the world.

Jerry travels all the time to stay connected with Yahoo! users so that he can constantly improve his website. He likes to frequent noodle shops and casual places where local residents like to go. Jerry sometimes takes two or three trips a month, making media appearances and meeting different people in the Internet business. Dealing with so many new people isn't always easy, and he's learned some important lessons along the way. He shared this tip in an interview with the online magazine *Salon*: "It helps a

ton when you learn people's names and don't butcher them when trying to pronounce them."

Jerry also feels it's important to know firsthand how other people use the Internet. For instance, in 2001 Jerry was still using a slow 28.8 modem because he wanted to experience what it was like to surf the Internet the way most people did.

In what little free time he has, Jerry golfs and watches wrestling, or he hangs out with his brother, Ken. They enjoy visiting their mother and loading up on her delicious cooking. Since Jerry and his wife Akiko both believe that people should give back to their community, the couple supports many arts and educational foundations.

CONCLUSION

Today Jerry Yang and David Filo are still close friends and business partners, continuing to live their dream at Yahoo! Neither has finished his Ph.D., but that is clearly not a problem! "[My particular Ph.D.] is now obsolete," Jerry told *Time* magazine. "But who knows? Being in school was very fun. Maybe I'll go back and do something else. I'm having a great time."

Is it feasible for two college friends to start an Internet company today? Some people might say it is much more difficult. The market is saturated with Internet companies; therefore it would require a strong public relations effort, including millions of dollars, to push a new company into the forefront. But if you have a great idea and have fun working on it, then anything is possible. The important thing is to work hard and follow your dreams, just the way Jerry Yang did. Succeeding at what you enjoy deserves a great, big yahoo!

Glossary

browser a software program that allows the user to connect to different sites on the Internet

bookmark the address of a website stored for easy retrieval

business plan a written document that describes the past, present, and future of a company. The plan tells what the business needs to do and how to do it.

database a collection of data arranged to make search and retrieval easy and quick

directory (or **online directory**) a database of online resources arranged hierarchically with multiple categories and sub-categories

"go public" an idiom that means to become publicly owned, by launching shares of stock that can be traded on the open market

hit a connection made to a website over the Internet

home page the web page that a browser automatically opens first; the opening page for a website

Internet a network of millions of connected computers and computer networks that share information

Internet service provider (ISP) a company that connects computers to the Internet

link highlighted words, phrases, or images that when clicked on go instantly to a website

search engine computer software for finding information on the web. To use a search engine, type in words or phrases related to the subject you are looking for. For example, if you are looking for horror movies, you might type in "horror," "horror movies," or even just "movies." The search engine will list many different links to choose from.

surfer one who casually looks at the Internet's numerous options

thesis a long paper that doctoral students must write in order to get a Ph.D. degree

Uniform Resource Locator (URL) the web address of a particular page on the Internet

venture capital companies firms that invest money in new companies or small ones wishing to expand

web page website

website a collection of documents on a World Wide Web (WWW) server

World Wide Web (WWW or the Web) the complete set of documents found on all Internet servers

Endnotes and Sources

Chapter 1

[1] www.goldsea.com

Chapter 2

[2] www.metroactive.com

[3] www.goldsea.com

[4] www.metroactive.com

Chapter 3

[5] www.soe.stanford.edu

[6] www.forbes.com

[7] www.soe.stanford.edu

[8] www.metroactive.com

[9] www.govtech.net

Chapter 4

[10] www.time.com

Additional sources:

www.yahoo.com

www.nytimes.com

www.salon.com

PC Magazine

Time magazine

Sherman, Josepha. *Jerry Yang and David Filo: Chief Yahoos of Yahoo!* Brookfield,
    Connecticut: Twenty-First Century Books, 2001.